To: Danica

Love: Papa & Grandma Cia

We hope you enjoy the stories in this book & how they relate to playing sports like you do. There's a letter to your parents on page 8.

REAL WINNERS

Written by Shaun Gayle   Illustrated by Patrick Owsley

VICTOR BOOKS

A DIVISION OF SCRIPTURE PRESS PUBLICATIONS INC.
USA CANADA ENGLAND

Book design: Scott Rattray
Illustrations © 1994, 1995 by Victor Books/SP Publications, Inc.
Text © 1994, 1995 by Shaun Gayle.
These stories are in print as individual books in
the "Shaun Gayle's Sports Tales" series.
All rights reserved. Printed in the U.S.A.
1 2 3 4 5 6 7 8 9 10 Printing/Year 99 98 97 96 95

VICTOR BOOKS
A division of SP Publications, Inc.
Wheaton, Illinois 60187

CONTENTS

A letter to parents   8

The Little Quarterback   9

Home Run Pete   31

Jill and the Hill   53

Jonathan McBoo   75

The Tennis Twins   97

The Golden Shoe Goalie   119

Dear Parents,

The influence of time is tremendous. What is heard and seen every day will have some type of effect on our kids. Whether our children spend time with us, or with others, we need to make sure it's in accordance with certain moral standards.

What was inexcusable ten years ago, today is commonplace—making the potential of tomorrow less than it should be. This can change by and through our children, but it's our responsibility to help them. We cannot know what our children may experience in our absence, but we can find comfort in using the opportunity to teach them beyond the mathematics and history lessons of a school curriculum. This can only happen through a commitment of time and effort.

We have to talk and listen to our kids: find out if they know what racism is; explain the importance of sacrifice and compassion; teach them the meaning of perseverance and faith; give them the moral foundation that seems to be disappearing in our society. We have to provide for them what we may not have had ourselves—realizing that anything we leave to chance is a chance we cannot afford to keep taking.

These books have specific themes with an emphasis on Christian values. Though the meaning of each book could be easily taken for granted or even overlooked, we should not minimize the importance of teaching our children lasting values that must overshadow the inevitable influences of time spent away from us.

I hope you and your children will read these books with each other and enjoy an investment of time well spent.

Shawn

The Little Quarterback

Once upon a time in a town in the midwest
There was a little school where football was best

It was the start of the season and the town was full of joy.
The fans were proud of their guys—each and every boy.

Now the game was just about to get under way,
So the players lined up and got ready to play.

The crowd went wild! People jumped up and down.
The cheerleaders, the band, almost the entire town!

The fans all shouted, "We're going to win big today!"
When out ran this little guy, ready to start the play.

The defense just stood there. They couldn't believe their eyes.
They looked over at the offense and standing tall was this little guy.

This little guy wasn't big, not very big at all.
Standing next to his team he looked three and a half feet tall.

"Now come on you guys! I know we can win."
He yelled to his offense to start the game again.

"We're going to get you, so don't try to run or hide,"
the defense shouted, trying to scare the little guy.

"You can't play against us. Just look at your size.
You're just way too small to play us big guys."

The little guy just smiled as he started the next play.
But the defense got tough and knocked him clear out of the way.

"We told you—you couldn't run and you couldn't hide.
Everyone knows you should just stand aside.

"This game is not for you. This game is for a man.
You're just a little quarterback who thinks he can."

The little guy jumped to his feet—and with a grin,
ran back to his team and said, "Let's try that again."

The defense snarled, "We're gonna get you. We mean it this time."
But the little guy ran with the ball, leaving the defense far behind.

As he ran down the field, almost completely alone,
He looked at the crowd as he made it to the end zone.

He noticed all the different faces of each and every fan,
And the strangest thing happened as he ran past the band.

He heard someone shout, "Wow! Give him a hand!
Way to go! Touchdown! Great play, you little man!"

Finally he stopped running and waved at the fans.
Everyone applauded—even the defense clapped their hands.

Everyone thought the little guy was way too small,
but he didn't let that stop him from playing football.

He said, "Size is not important, and it won't make you a man,
It's what's in your heart that tells you if you can't or if you can."

At last the game was over and both teams left the field.
The defense stopped the little guy and offered him a deal.

"Come and play for us, and we'll make you the best...
You'll be the biggest star ever... far better than the rest."

The little guy said, "No thanks. You don't really need me,
Good players are out there, whatever size they may be.

"Don't judge anyone on just what you see.
Find out who they are and what they can be.

"God gives us talents that make us special in our own way.
We can all honor Him in how we work and how we play."

Time passed, and soon the next big game got under way.
The crowd cheered loud and clear as the teams ran out to play.

As the visiting team stood there, next to the football,
their players looked different—some were skinny, some were small.

And this time around there was no problem at all,
with kids of all shapes who loved to play football.

No one can really say what's possible for you.
Only God knows for sure what great things you can do.

Home Run Pete

It was the time of year when baseball season came around.
There was a team of boys who were the best in town.

There were "Big Hands Willie" and "String Bean Joe,"
a short guy named "Stretch" and a tall guy named "Mo."

Each time they played, they usually won.
These guys played hard and had lots of fun.

There was one player who was the best of them all.
He played bigger than life—like he was ten feet tall!

He'd walk up to the plate and stick out his chest,
look at the crowd and shout "Who's the best?"

The fans would clap and stamp their feet.
They'd stand and shout, "It's Home Run Pete!"

The players all enjoyed winning the games,
but it was tough to play with a guy of Pete's fame.

"You're great," Mo said, "and we like what you do,
but don't forget about the team because we play too."

"He's right," added Big Hands. "We also want to be known.
We have to play together; you can't play this game alone.

But Pete was king, and this was his way.
He expected all the cheers on each and every day.

"I don't play with you guys; you guys play with me!
I'm the best on this team, and that's easy to see."

The guys got upset. Stretch said, "This won't do.
We don't like your way. We want to be cheered too."

As the season went by, Pete's problem was clear.
Finally it was time for the last game of the year.

During the ninth inning when it was late,
Home Run Pete stood proudly at the plate.

But in a matter of seconds silence ended the shouts,
because their home run champ had somehow struck out.

The fans screamed, "Pete, how could you be that way?"
They didn't understand this just wasn't his day.

Here was their champ who had always stood tall.
The fans just couldn't believe he had missed the ball!

The guys now knew it was up to them to win.
When Pete struck out, it seemed like the end.

The game was close but the guys pulled it through,
Thanks to String Bean and Big Hands, just to name a few.

The crowd roared, "Yea! Yea! You guys are great!"
as the team lined up across home plate.

Each player stepped forward as he heard his name,
thinking, *what a great feeling to play this game.*

And at the end of the line was Home Run Pete,
quietly standing there remembering his defeat.

But the team surrounded Pete that day.
They cheered and clapped and said it was OK.

"You guys are good," Home Run Pete did say.
"You all deserve more credit for the way you play."

"It's tough to play with pride," Stretch told Pete.
"It's not good when you win or when you get beat."

From that point on at the end of each game,
Pete supported his team and shared the fame.

The fans still clapped and stamped their feet,
cheering for the team, not just Home Run Pete.

Jill and the Hill

Once upon a time there was a girl named Jill,
who loved to run track and lived on a hill.

Everyone watched what Jill could do.
She ran so fast and wore just one shoe.

Family and friends stopped by all the time,
wanting to talk to a star in her prime.

During track meets they yelled so loud,
Jill ran even faster and felt very proud.

Now the biggest meet of the season was due,
and everyone wanted to see the girl with one shoe.

"It's the greatest race ever," the coach said with a thrill.
"We're going to race to the top of that hill."

The news spread fast throughout the town.
They all wanted to see the fastest girl around.

The students all knew she would do great things,
running so fast—as if she had wings.

Jill was good and enjoyed being cheered,
but the day before the meet, something happened that she feared.

While training on the hill, Jill slipped and fell,
and when she got up, she just didn't feel well.

Jill looked at her foot as it turned black and blue.
She had sprained her ankle because she wore one shoe.

The coach told her it would be all right,
that even without Jill the team could put up a good fight.

Jill became so upset that she couldn't compete,
she wouldn't eat and she wouldn't sleep.

Her problem was not being able to run,
she thought people might think she was no longer fun.

She was afraid her friends would no longer hang around
if she wasn't a star or the most popular girl in town.

The meet was over and Jill's team did lose.
Some fans cheered, and some fans booed.

It was easy to see the sadness on Jill's face,
thinking she lost her friends because she couldn't race.

But in the end Jill's friends still stopped by.
They brought her cake and candy and some apple pie.

"You made me feel so special when I ran," said Jill.
"I was afraid you'd all leave if I couldn't run the hill."

Her friends said, "We wouldn't leave you just for having a bad day,
whether you have one shoe or two, a true friend would stay."

Jill thought her friends only cared because she could run,
because she was a town star, and because she seemed fun.

So whether we get candy or apple pies,
God wants us to love with our hearts, and not our eyes.

A short time later Jill ran up the hill again,
not worried this time about losing a true friend.

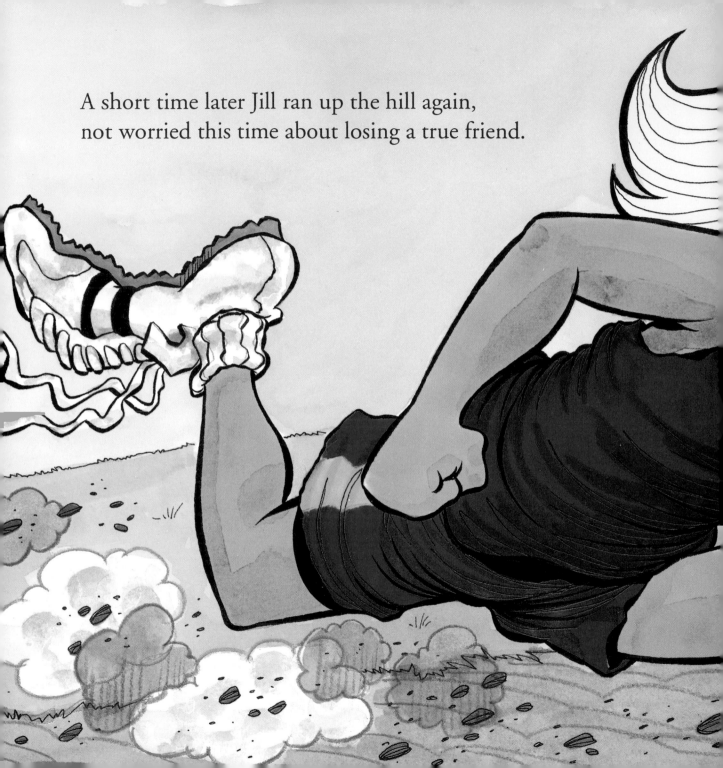

Jonathan McBoo

Not long ago in a school you might know,
was a boy so tall you could see him grow.

He didn't want to play basketball for a team,
though he'd be great, being so tall and lean.

The coaches would all greet him and say,
"Come shoot this basketball. Show us how well you play."

But the boy would just stand there and smile to himself,
knowing basketball might easily bring him fame and wealth.

The team got angry! They couldn't believe this guy,
being so tall he could almost touch the sky.

"Why don't you play with us? Are you afraid you won't win?"
said the guys on the team trying to get the boy to join in.

"I don't like this game, and I don't want to play,"
the boy said—wanting to get on with his day.

"Without basketball, there's no need for you,"
the guys told the boy who was seven-foot-two.

Well, the guys played anyway in the school's gym,
but the ball got stuck when it bounced off the rim.

"Oh, no!" shouted the boys, "What will we do?"
while the ball sat on a beam, just barely in view.

The principal came to the gym and said with a frown,
"That's the only ball we have, so we need to get it down."

The team, the principal—and now the janitor too—
all stood there wondering what they could do.

"I know," said the principal, pointing down the hall,
"Get that new student, the one who hates basketball."

Someone asked, "How can he help us get the ball?
If he won't use his height, he'll be no good at all."

In walked the boy, and he said, "Can I help you?"
The principal told them, "Meet Jonathan, Jonathan McBoo."

The guys said with a laugh, "So your name is Jonathan, Jonathan McBo
If you can't play basketball, then what can you do?"

He looked up at the ball, and then at the floor.
He counted each guy, then walked out the door.

The guys said, "We told you he was no good at all.
There's no way he could help us get our ball."'

The players looked unhappy; their fun was done that day.
Until they noticed Jonathan was back with more to say.

He yelled, "Not even I can jump that high.
We'll have to make a pyramid from the floor to the sky."

Ten students followed as he walked through the gym door
and they all lined themselves up across the gym floor.

Three minutes later, the pyramid stood tall.
And at the top was a cheerleader who easily got the ball.

The principal laughed and said to McBoo,
"Playing basketball is great, but thinking is good too."

McBoo said, "Basketball is great if you want to play.
There are just other things I want to do with my day."

"I want everyone to like me for being me,
not for what they hope I am or think I should be."

The guys agreed, "Jonathan, maybe you're right.
It really doesn't matter if you choose to use your height."

"That's not the point," the principal said.
"Try using your skill and *also* your head."

"Some of our talents are easy to see,
but if we use all of God's gifts, the better we'll be."

The Tennis Twins

Somewhere, in the big city during warm summer nights,
city kids gathered to play tennis under the lights.

The sounds of the city were so distinct and clear
the subway and the trains always seemed easy to hear.

The games the kids played were fun in their own way—
like stickball and basketball which they played each day.

But tennis was a game they could play all the time—
in the morning or afternoon even without sunshine.

The kids loved to play those games in the street,
but tennis at night helped them avoid the summer heat.

Tennis was really fun, and everyone loved to win.
The kids liked the competition and no one ever gave in.

Even though they weren't the best players in the world,
the best of the group was this one little boy and little girl.

They were in many matches and had lots of wins.
They played great together because they were twins.

One night, as usual, while they were having a good time,
two new boys boasted, "We're the best you'll ever find."

Everyone watched the twins and the boys play,
but the twins were too good in almost every way.

The twins had soundly beaten them three games to one,
and while they were doing it, they seemed to have fun.

The kids told the twins how tough they were to beat,
but it was the little boy who claimed he caused their defeat.

"We play well together as you can probably see,
but the reason we beat everyone is because of me.

"Everyone knows a boy is better than any girl.
Everyone knows that–everyone in the whole wide world!"

But the little girl said, "No way. That's just not true.
You're not better than me. In fact, I'm better than you.

"Just because you're a boy doesn't mean you're better than me.
Girls can do what boys do and even be what boys want to be."

"I can be a fire fighter, an astronaut, or even a truck driver too.
Girls can be what they want to be and do whatever they want to do."

The little boy said, "I don't know what you can be,
but I do know in tennis you can't beat me."

"You're my sister and you're good—yes, that is true.
If you think you're better, let's play and I'll show you."

As they began playing, all the kids watched the court—
enjoying their effort and the way they played the sport.

The little girl was fearless as she played that game,
proving to her brother their talent was not the same.

The kids began to laugh. Even the little girl started to grin,
realizing the little boy was losing, and she was going to win.

One boy said, "Hey! You can't possibly lose to a girl!
That's a terrible thing—the worst thing in the world."

But she looked at her brother and noticed his face,
his look of embarrassment, his look of disgrace.

She wanted to show her brother something—without the shame,
knowing his feelings were more important than any tennis game.

So she stopped the match before it was done,
as they both understood she'd have easily won.

She said to her brother, "I just wanted you to see
just by being a boy doesn't mean you're better than me."

The game was over and they'd both played really well
proving talent is what matters—not being female or male.

The Golden Shoe Goalie

It was the time of summer, in a nearby neighborhood,
at a soccer field behind homes of brick and wood.

As usual, that morning the soccer field was packed
with parents and their poodles and kids having snacks.

And the families had all gathered—as they did each Saturday
talking with the neighbors and watching kids play.

Yet this day of soccer was far different than the rest.
The Golden Shoe Goalie was coming and she was the best.

She was said to be swift and quick as a cat.
She once kicked the ball so hard, it actually went flat.

They'd never seen this girl before, but they all knew her name.
She was legendary for wearing shoes of gold, and never losing a game.

The goalie and her family were new to the neighborhood,
so the neighbors prepared a welcome like good neighbors should.

And as the family car pulled up near the fence by the gate,
everyone ran over to meet the golden shoe great.

The goalie's family stood there as the crowd came near,
but their excitement turned to whispers instead of cheers.

"Hey, wait a minute," one man said. "This can't be.
You can't be the Golden Shoe Goalie we came to see."

"We want our kids to have fun and not make a fuss.
We don't think you belong here; you're just not like us."

The Goalie's father said, "We're different. Yes, that's true.
We're also a family who loves soccer, just like you."

"If you don't want us here, we're still going to stay.
We can always go elsewhere when it's time to play."

The families kept talking in small groups, one-on-one,
too upset to notice that a game had just begun.

They soon heard shouts of joy and loud cheers of fun,
because the kids didn't care what their folks had done.

The parents all walked over and sat in the stands,
watching their kids play and even cheering like fans.

They all stared at the Golden Shoe Goalie as she played the game,
and it was easy to see why her talent brought her fame.

She was graceful and swift as they had heard before.
Though the kids tried their best, no one there could score.

The families were amazed that this goalie was so good.
They now wanted her to live near their homes of brick and wood.

"Maybe we were wrong," Mrs. Witman told the goalie's dad.
"We hope you'll be our neighbors. Sorry we made you mad!"

"We weren't welcome here until you saw my daughter play,"
replied her dad. "That's not a good reason to want us to stay."

As the parents talked, all the kids came over and stood.
The Golden Shoe Goalie pointed to the houses of brick and wood.

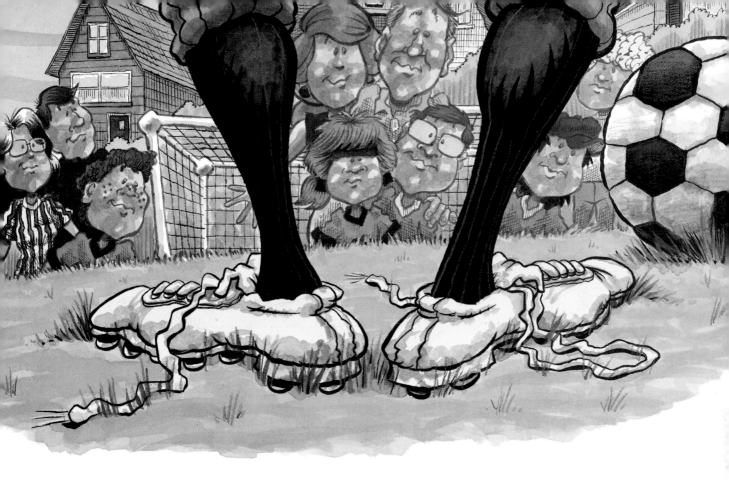

"This neighborhood is nice, and I enjoyed the game.
But how would you treat us if I didn't have this fame?"

"I don't want to be accepted because of what I do.
We should be treated as equals, the same as all of you."

"I played with the other kids, and we all enjoyed the game.
It didn't seem to matter if we were different or the same."

"These kids didn't see color, culture, or race.
They just saw another kid, another smiling face."

"We parents tried to teach what should and shouldn't be,
but it was our kids who taught us how to live in harmony."

The goalie and the kids played together day and night.
They all had a great time, (though they'd sometimes fight).

It was through those times that helped their parents agree
that the only differences that matter are the ones we can't see.

"It's not our appearance, or our money or our fame.
It's our hearts that tell us if we're different or the same."

"If we hadn't tried to live together, we'd never have understood
that all types of people can live together in a neighborhood."

"We should never just see the color of someone's skin.
It's their character that matters; it's what's inside of them."

"In God's eyes we all look the same
regardless of our looks, regardless of our name."

"We should live our lives with respect and love,
caring for one another and honoring God above."

Shaun Gayle is a veteran NFL football player with a "heart for kids." A graduate of Ohio State University with a degree in education, Shaun Gayle was with the Chicago Bears from 1982 to 1994 and then joined the San Diego Chargers. He was captain of the victorious 1985 Super Bowl XX team and in 1984 was the recipient of the Brian Piccolo Award.

Patrick Owsley holds a B.A. in illustration from Columbia College in Chicago. He has done cartoon illustrations for magazines, advertising, greeting cards, coloring books, and comic books; and currently works on staff as an "in-house" letterer for Malibu Comics Entertainment. He lives in Southern California with his wife Kristine and two daughters.